The Cape Malay
Illustrated Cookbook

Dhania

Onion

Aniseed

Garlic

Chilli

Mint

Cinnamon

Bay Leaves

Cloves

The Cape Malay
Illustrated Cookbook

Faldela Williams

Illustrated by Liz Mills

First published in 2007 by Struik Publishers
(a division of New Holland Publishing (South Africa) (Pty) Ltd)
Cape Town * London * Sydney * Auckland
www.struik.co.za

Cornelis Struik House, 80 McKenzie Street, Cape Town 8001, South Africa
Garfield House, 86–88 Edgware Road, London W2 2EA, United Kingdom
Unit 1, 66 Gibbes Street, Chatswood, NSW 2067, Australia
218 Lake Road, Northcote, Auckland, New Zealand

New Holland Publishing is a member of Johnnic Communications Ltd

1 3 5 7 9 10 8 6 4 2

PUBLISHING MANAGER: Linda de Villiers
MANAGING EDITOR: Cecilia Barfield
EDITOR: Joy Clack
DESIGNER: Beverley Dodd
ILLUSTRATOR: Liz Mills
PROOFREADER: Irma van Wyk

Reproduction by Hirt & Carter Cape (Pty) Ltd
Printed and bound by Craft Print International Pte Limited, Singapore

ISBN 978 1 77007 405 7

www.imagesofafrica.co.za

IMAGES OF AFRICA
PHOTO LIBRARY

Over 40 000 unique African images available to purchase from our image bank at www.imagesofafrica.co.za

Contents

INTRODUCTION 7

CONVERSION TABLES 7

SNACKS 8

FISH AND SEAFOOD 16

CHICKEN 26

MEAT 32

VEGETABLES AND ACCOMPANIMENTS 46

DESSERTS 54

BISCUITS, BREADS AND CAKES 62

INDEX 80

Introduction

As a young girl peeling potatoes in my grandmother's kitchen in District Six I could never have imagined that I would be invited around the world to cook at festivals, grand hotels, ambassadors' residences and convention centres.

Since the publication of my first cookbook in 1988 there have been a lot of changes in our society. Food is also part of those changes, especially since Cape Town has become the melting pot of the whole of South Africa. The recipes compiled for this book are and always will be very popular for many more years to come. Always remember that Cape Malay cooking is very flexible.

It is better to make the curry or bredie (stew) well in advance, as the spices take time to develop and impart their flavour to the food. Spices should be used as fresh as possible. Most spices can be bought whole and, when needed, can be toasted in a pan for about 2 minutes, and then ground in a coffee grinder. Store spices in airtight jars to keep them fresh.

All the ingredients used are readily available from supermarkets and spice shops. The red bolus for Fawzia's Soetkoekies (page 63) is available from pharmacies.

BISMILLAH!

Conversion Tables

METRIC	US CUPS	IMPERIAL
5 ml	1 tsp	³⁄₁₆ fl oz
15 ml	1 Tbsp	½ fl oz
60 ml	4 Tbsp (¼ cup)	2 fl oz
80 ml	⅓ cup	2¾ fl oz
125 ml	½ cup	4½ fl oz
160 ml	⅔ cup	5½ fl oz
200 ml	¾ cup or ⅘ cup	7 fl oz
250 ml	1 cup	9 fl oz

METRIC	IMPERIAL
100 g	3½ oz
250 g	9 oz
500 g	1 lb
750 g	1¾ lb
1 kg	2¼ lb

Snacks

Dhaltjies

These chilli bites are the perfect party snack. You can vary this recipe by adding
250 ml whole kernel corn instead of spinach, or by adding a grated potato.

250 ml pea or chana flour
30 ml self-raising flour
1 onion, grated or finely chopped
5 ml ground jeera (cumin)
5 ml ground koljana (coriander)
10 ml crushed dried chillies or 2 fresh green
chillies, finely chopped
5 ml salt

3 ml turmeric (borrie)
½ bunch chopped green dhania leaves
(fresh coriander)
1 small Granny Smith apple, grated
a few spinach leaves, shredded
5 ml baking powder
500 ml sunflower oil for deep-frying

Sift pea and self-raising flour into a fairly large mixing bowl. Add remaining ingredients, except baking powder and oil, and mix with sufficient water to make a thick, lumpy batter. Stir in baking powder just before frying.

Heat oil in a deep frying pan. Drop heaped teaspoons of batter into hot oil and fry until lightly browned, about 5 minutes. Turn over and brown other side. Drain on paper towel or in a colander. Serve hot.

VARIATION
Bhajias: Instead of shredding spinach leaves, break into about 5 cm squares and dip in batter. Shallow-fry on both sides in hot oil until crisp, about 6 minutes in all. Drain well on paper towel and serve.

Haddock Balls

MAKES 30

An unusual savoury snack or light luncheon dish, adapted to the Malay style.

500 g smoked haddock fillets
water
2 large potatoes, cooked and mashed
20 ml finely chopped fresh parsley
5 ml ground white or black pepper
1 egg, lightly beaten
dried breadcrumbs
sunflower oil for deep-frying

Poach haddock in water to cover for about 10 minutes, drain well and flake fish. Combine with mashed potatoes, parsley and pepper, and roll into balls. Dip in beaten egg, then roll in breadcrumbs. Heat oil in a deep pan and deep-fry haddock balls until browned and crisp, about 10 minutes.

Serve hot as a snack, or as a light meal with chips and a salad.

Egg and Shrimp on Toast

SERVES 2

This makes a very special breakfast treat.

4 large eggs, well beaten
15 ml milk
30 ml sunflower oil
250 g shrimp, shelled and deveined
2 ml salt
5 ml chilli powder

Combine eggs and milk. Heat oil in a frying pan and fry shrimps until they turn pink, 5–10 minutes. Add salt and chilli powder, stir, and then add milk and egg mixture. Cook until eggs are set but still soft and moist, about 5 minutes.

Serve on hot buttered toast or use as a filling for snackwiches.

Spicy Kebaabs

Kebaabs are spicy meatballs fried until golden brown.
Serve with a tangy fruit chutney or chilli sauce for easy entertaining.

500 g steak mince
2 slices stale bread, soaked in water
15 ml sunflower oil
1 onion, grated or finely chopped
5 ml crushed garlic
2 green chillies, finely chopped
10 ml ground jeera (cumin)
5 ml ground koljana (coriander)
5 ml salt
1 egg
300 ml sunflower oil for frying

Rinse mince and leave in colander to drain. Squeeze moisture out of bread. Heat 15 ml oil in frying pan and add onion, spices and salt. Stir-fry for 5 minutes. Mix mince, bread, onion mixture and egg in a mixing bowl until well-blended.

Form into small balls and fry in heated oil until lightly browned, about 5 minutes. Turn over and brown other side.

Spear with toothpicks and serve.

Savoury Pies

MAKES 50

A favourite snack that can be served at weddings or at a buffet supper. For a more substantial filling,
add 100 g uncooked vermicelli to mince mixture just before adding the sago.

1 kg ready-made puff pastry
1 egg, beaten

STEAK FILLING
500 g steak, cut into small cubes
1 large onion, finely chopped
15 ml sunflower oil
5 ml crushed garlic

5 ml salt
5 ml ground black pepper
2 ml grated nutmeg
2 ml ground cloves
5 ml crushed dried chillies or chilli powder
100 ml sago soaked in 125 ml water for
　15 minutes
3 hard-boiled eggs, grated

Filling: Wash steak and drain well. Braise onion in heated oil until golden, 5–10 minutes. Add steak and cook for about 30 minutes, stirring, over medium heat. Add spices and cook a further 15 minutes, stirring frequently. Drain sago and add to steak mixture. Cook, stirring, until sago is transparent, about 10 minutes. Leave to cool.

Cut out pastry rounds, 7.5 cm in diameter or 7.5 cm squares, and place about 10 ml steak mixture in centre of half of them. Top with a little grated egg. Place remaining pastry rounds or squares on top and seal edges. Brush with beaten egg, arrange on a baking sheet and bake at 200 °C for 15 minutes. Reduce temperature to 180 °C and bake a further 10 minutes, or until pastry is golden brown.

FREEZER TIP
Freeze unbaked savoury pies in a suitable container. There is no need to thaw them before baking. Brush with a little beaten egg, arrange on a baking sheet and bake as directed above for 20 minutes.

Fish and Seafood

Kingklip and Prawn Paella

SERVES 10–12

1 kg uncooked long grain rice
1 kg kingklip fillets, cut into small pieces
1 kg prawns, cut and deveined
3 onions, thinly sliced
sunflower oil
1 green pepper, seeded and chopped
1 red pepper, seeded and chopped
200 g button mushrooms, sliced
Tabasco® sauce

salt
125 g butter

MARINADE
60 ml chilli sauce
10 ml garlic paste
10 ml pickle masala
5 ml salt
5 ml Tabasco® sauce

Cook rice in salted boiling water until tender, about 20 minutes. Drain and set aside.

Combine all marinade ingredients and marinate kingklip and prawns for about 30 minutes. Meanwhile, fry onions in a little oil in a very deep frying pan or wok until golden, 5–10 minutes. Add peppers and fry a further 10 minutes, add mushrooms and fry a further 5 minutes. Remove from pan and set aside. Add about 15 ml oil to frying pan. Transfer marinated kingklip and prawn mixture to frying pan and stir-fry for 10 minutes, or until prawns turns pink. Layer ingredients in a large saucepan as follows: first, about one-third rice, then half onion and mushroom mixture, then half kingklip and prawn mixture. Continue layering until all ingredients have been used up. Sprinkle each layer with a few drops of Tabasco®. Season with salt, dot with butter and steam, covered, over medium heat for 30 minutes.

VARIATION
Mussels and calamari make good additions to this paella. Marinate the mussels and calamari with the kingklip and prawns.

Fried Kabeljou with Mushroom, Tomato and Pepper Sauce

SERVES 4

A quick and easy family dish.

800 g kabeljou (cob) or other line fish fillets, cut into portions
salt and freshly ground black pepper
150 ml sunflower oil

MUSHROOM, TOMATO AND PEPPER SAUCE
1 onion, finely chopped
50 ml sunflower oil

1 green pepper, seeded and sliced
2 tomatoes, skinned and chopped
200 g mushrooms, sliced
1 small fresh green chilli, chopped or 5 ml crushed dried chillies
5 ml dried mixed herbs
15 ml sugar
salt

SAUCE: Sauté onion in hot oil until golden, add green pepper and simmer for 5–10 minutes. Add tomatoes and simmer, covered, for 20 minutes. Add mushrooms, chilli, herbs and sugar. Simmer, covered, for a further 10 minutes, then add salt to taste.

While sauce is simmering, prepare fish. Season fish lightly with salt and pepper. Heat oil in a frying pan and fry fish on both sides over medium heat until lightly browned and cooked through, 10–15 minutes. Drain on paper towel and then place on a bed of white rice on serving platter. Pour sauce over fish.

COOK'S TIP
To test if fish is done, flake one end with a fork. If done, the flesh should be white and flake easily.

Smoorsnoek with Cabbage

SERVES 8

*A traditional dish that goes back a long way. In Malay households fish is
generally served on a Monday after the rich spicy foods eaten on the weekend.*

1 kg dried salted snoek	5 ml crushed garlic
water	1 dried red chilli or 5 ml crushed dried chillies
2 onions, thinly sliced	5 ml sugar
30 ml sunflower oil	4 potatoes, quartered
1 medium cabbage, shredded	

Soak snoek in water for 1 hour. Drain, cover with fresh water and boil until cooked, about 15 minutes.
Meanwhile, braise onions in heated oil until quite brown, about 10 minutes. Add cabbage and garlic, and cook,
covered, until cabbage is lightly browned, about 15 minutes. Add chilli and sugar. Add potatoes and simmer,
covered, until potatoes are cooked, about 15 minutes.

   Drain and flake snoek. Add to cabbage mixture and simmer for 15 minutes, or until flavours are well-blended.
Serve with white rice and vegetable or lemon atjar.

VARIATIONS

Use 2 x 400 g cans smoorsnoek (available at supermarkets) instead of dried snoek. Add salt to taste.
Use 2 x 200 g cans tuna, drained, instead of dried snoek. Add salt if needed.

Fish Frikkadels

An economical dish, which can also be served with dhal curry.

2 slices stale white bread	5 ml salt
water	2 ml ground nutmeg
500 g minced hake or other firm white fish	10 ml ground jeera (cumin)
5 ml crushed garlic	2 ml ground white pepper
1 onion, grated	5 ml crushed dried chillies
1 firm ripe tomato, grated or finely chopped	50 ml chopped fresh parsley
1 egg	400 ml sunflower oil

Soak bread in water for 5 minutes, then squeeze out all moisture. Add to fish with remaining ingredients, except oil, and mix to bind well. Shape into patties and shallow-fry in medium-hot oil for about 5 minutes on each side, or until lightly browned. Serve hot with white rice, blatjang or mushroom, tomato and pepper sauce (page 18).

VARIATION
Use 2 x 200 g cans tuna, drained and flaked, in place of minced hake.

Pickled Fish

Pickled fish is a dish I always associate with the festive season.
Any firm-fleshed white fish may be used instead of kabeljou or yellowtail.

2 kg kabeljou (cob) or yellowtail fillets,
cut into portions
salt and ground white pepper
250 ml sunflower oil

CURRY SAUCE
15 ml sunflower oil
3 large onions, thinly sliced

200 ml white grape vinegar
50 ml water
30 ml sugar or to taste
5 ml turmeric (borrie)
10 ml curry powder
5 ml chilli powder
5 bay leaves
salt

Season fish portions with salt and pepper. Heat oil in deep frying pan and fry fish for 5 minutes on each side, or until medium brown. Remove from oil and drain on paper towel.

Sauce: Heat oil in separate pan, add onions, vinegar, water, sugar and spices, and cook until well blended, 10–15 minutes. Add salt to taste. Place drained fish slices in a deep dish and cover with hot onion mixture. Refrigerate, covered, for 24 hours before use to allow flavours to develop. Serve cold with bread.

Tuna Biryani

SERVES 4–6

A quick and easy yet substantial meal to prepare instead of fish biryani.

100 ml sunflower oil
3 potatoes, sliced
50 g butter
1 large onion, thinly sliced
10 ml pickle masala
5 ml whole jeera (cumin)

250 g frozen mixed vegetables
750 ml cooked long grain rice
2 x 200 g cans tuna chunks
100 ml hot water
3 hard-boiled eggs, quartered

Heat oil in a frying pan and fry potato slices for about 5 minutes on each side, or until golden brown. Drain and set aside. Melt butter in a saucepan and fry onion until golden, 5–10 minutes. Add spices and mixed vegetables, and cook a further 10 minutes. Layer 375 ml rice in a large saucepan, top with tuna, potatoes, mixed vegetables, remaining rice and hot water. Cook covered for 15 minutes on medium heat. Serve garnished with hard-boiled egg quarters.

MICROWAVE TIP
Layer prepared ingredients in a casserole dish as described above and microwave, covered, on medium (50%) for 10 minutes, to finish cooking the biryani.

Chicken

Braised Masala Chicken

SERVES 6

A very tasty, traditional dish, also called gesmoorde hoender.

12 portions chicken
10 ml crushed garlic
7 ml crushed fresh ginger
5 ml crushed dried chillies
10 ml ground jeera (cumin)
10 ml roasted masala
5 whole cloves

10 ml peri-peri sauce
7 ml salt
30 ml sunflower oil
2 onions, finely chopped
1 tomato, grated
1 green pepper, seeded and finely sliced
2 potatoes, peeled and quartered

Wash and drain chicken. Mix together garlic, ginger, chillies, jeera, masala, cloves, peri-peri sauce and salt. Rub into chicken portions and set aside. Heat oil in a saucepan and braise onions until golden brown, 5–10 minutes. Add tomato and green pepper, and cook for about 10 minutes. Add chicken and cook for about 20 minutes. Add potatoes and simmer for 15 minutes, or until potatoes are soft. Serve with savoury rice and a green salad.

Pineapple Peri-Peri Chicken

SERVES 5

This dish has a tangy pineapple sauce which blends well with chicken.

5 ml salt
10 ml crushed garlic
10 portions chicken
30 ml cake flour

5 ml peri-peri powder
1 x 440 g can pineapple rings, syrup drained
and reserved

Rub salt and garlic into chicken portions. Mix flour and peri-peri, and sprinkle over chicken on both sides. Arrange chicken portions in a greased ovenproof dish and pour syrup reserved from pineapple over the top. Bake at 180 °C for about 1 hour, or until lightly browned, spooning pineapple syrup over chicken about twice and turning chicken over halfway through cooking time. Arrange pineapple rings over chicken and bake a further 10–15 minutes. Serve with savoury rice and a salad.

Chicken Curry

SERVES 6–8

An all-time favourite.

1.5 kg chicken, cut into portions
2 large onions, thinly sliced
30 ml sunflower oil
10 ml garlic and ginger paste
5 ml turmeric (borrie)
10 ml ground jeera (cumin)
10 ml ground koljana (coriander)
5 cardamom pods

3 pieces stick cinnamon
10 ml roasted masala
5 whole cloves
10 ml salt
200 ml water
2 large tomatoes, chopped and puréed
3 medium potatoes, peeled and quartered

Wash and drain chicken. Meanwhile, braise onions in heated oil until golden brown, 5–10 minutes. Add chicken to onions. Add garlic and ginger paste and rest of spices and 100 ml water, and then simmer, covered, for 20 minutes, or until well blended. Add tomatoes and simmer a further 10 minutes. Add remaining water and potatoes, and simmer a further 10–15 minutes, or until potatoes are cooked. Serve with rice or Malay rotis (page 47) and tomato and onion salad (page 51).

Meat

Spicy Lamb Chops

SERVES 5

A casserole of lamb baked in a spicy yoghurt sauce.

1 kg lamb loin chops	5 ml roasted masala
200 g button mushrooms	10 ml crushed garlic
8 baby potatoes, peeled	10 ml crushed fresh ginger
200 ml plain yoghurt	10 ml ground jeera (cumin)
7 ml salt	5 ml ground koljana (coriander)
2 green chillies, finely chopped	30 ml sunflower oil

Place lamb chops, mushrooms and potatoes in a greased ovenproof dish. Combine yoghurt with remaining ingredients and pour over ingredients in dish. Bake at 200 °C for 30–45 minutes, or until meat is cooked and sauce is brown and bubbling. Serve with a green salad and garlic bread.

Denningvleis

There is no other name in any language for this popular Malay dish. At first glance it looks like lamb stew,
but when eaten it has a lingering, sweet-sour and spicy undertone.

1 kg leg of lamb, deboned
10 ml sunflower oil
2 large onions, sliced

MARINADE
10 ml crushed garlic
5 ml crushed dried red chillies
7 ml salt
3 ml ground black pepper
3 bay leaves
5 whole allspice
3 whole cloves
25 ml sugar, or to taste
20 ml brown grape vinegar

Wash meat very well and then cut into 5 cm chunks. Combine the marinade ingredients and coat meat with it. Set aside for 1 hour.

Heat oil in large saucepan, add onions and cook until nicely browned. Add meat and cook, covered, over medium heat until meat is well done, 45–60 minutes. If meat gets too dry, add a little water (no more than 125 ml).

Serve meat hot with boiled squash, mashed potatoes and almond yellow rice (page 48).

COOK'S TIP
Traditionally, tamarind was used instead of vinegar for the marinade. Soak 30 ml tamarind in 60 ml water, squeeze out juice and add the juice to marinade ingredients.

Bobotie

*This light-textured, curried meat loaf topped with a golden savoury custard
is one of the most well-known Malay dishes.*

2 slices stale white bread	20 ml lemon juice
water	100 ml seedless raisins (optional)
30 ml sunflower oil	30 ml sugar
1 onion, thinly sliced	1 egg
10 ml crushed garlic	
2 ml ground cloves	TOPPING
10 ml curry powder	2 eggs, lightly beaten
5 ml turmeric (borrie)	150 ml milk
10 ml roasted masala	2 ml salt
5 ml salt	4 bay leaves or lemon leaves for garnish
500 g steak mince	

Soak bread in water for 10 minutes, then squeeze dry. Heat oil in a large saucepan and braise onion until golden, 5–10 minutes. Add garlic, spices, salt and steak mince, and cook, covered, for about 15 minutes. Add lemon juice, raisins and sugar, and cook to combine well, about 10 minutes. Remove from heat, add bread and egg and mix well.

Spoon mixture into well-greased ovenproof dish and bake at 160 °C for 30 minutes. Remove from oven. Beat eggs, milk and salt well and pour over bobotie. Add bay or lemon leaves, and bake a further 10–15 minutes at 180 °C. Serve with almond yellow rice (page 48) and boiled vegetables.

Sosatie Chops

SERVES 6

This is a modern version of the traditional sosatie. It is superb, as it's oil free. Try it.

1 kg lamb chops
2 large onions, thinly sliced

MARINADE
10 ml crushed garlic
3 bay leaves
3 whole cloves
5 ml turmeric (borrie)
30 ml curry powder
10 ml roasted masala
45 ml sugar
7 ml salt
60 ml lemon juice or white grape vinegar

Combine the marinade ingredients and marinate chops for 1 hour.

Place meat and marinade in a saucepan with onions and cook, covered, over medium heat for 45–60 minutes, or until meat is tender. Serve with boiled squash and mashed potatoes.

Spicy Cottage Pie

500 g steak mince
1 large onion, thinly sliced
10 ml crushed garlic
5 ml ground black pepper
7 ml salt
2 ml ground cloves
2 ml grated nutmeg
50 ml sago, soaked in 100 ml water for 15 minutes

3 hard-boiled eggs, sliced
1 egg, well beaten

MASHED POTATOES
500 g potatoes, peeled and cubed
50 g butter
100 ml hot milk
5 ml baking powder

Combine steak mince and onion in a saucepan and braise slowly, covered, for 30 minutes. Add garlic, pepper, salt, cloves and nutmeg, and cook a further 10 minutes. Add sago and cook over medium heat for about 15 minutes, or until sago is translucent.

Mashed potatoes: Cook the potatoes in salted boiling water for 15–20 minutes, or until soft enough to mash. Drain off excess water. Add the butter, milk and baking powder, and mash until soft and fluffy.

Transfer mince from saucepan to a greased ovenproof dish. Layer hard-boiled egg slices on top and cover with mashed potatoes. Pour over beaten egg and bake at 200 °C for 15 minutes. Serve with lightly steamed vegetables and beetroot and onion salad.

VARIATION
Use 500 g cubed steak instead of steak mince. Add 15 minutes extra cooking time before adding sago.

Tomato Bredie

SERVES 6

Ripe, red tomatoes are best for this dish. If you have to use canned tomatoes or less than ripe tomatoes, add 15 ml tomato paste for extra flavour.

2 large onions, thinly sliced
30 ml sunflower oil
1 kg mutton knuckles, chopped
4 large ripe tomatoes, skinned and grated or puréed

10 ml crushed garlic
7 ml salt
5 ml crushed dried red chillies
4 medium potatoes, quartered
45 ml sugar, or to taste

Braise onions in heated oil until golden, 5–10 minutes. Add meat and simmer over medium heat for 30–40 minutes, stirring from time to time. Add tomatoes, crushed garlic, salt and chilli, and simmer a further 20 minutes. Add potatoes and cook until tender, about 15 minutes. Add sugar and cook a further 5 minutes. Serve with white rice.

COOK'S TIP
Add sugar last, as the potatoes take a long time to cook if sugar is added first.

MICROWAVE TIP
Microwave quartered potatoes with 50 ml water for 5 minutes on full power (100%). Add to bredie and cook for 5 minutes before adding sugar. This will reduce cooking time by about 15 minutes.

Mutton Curry

This mutton curry has a thick, tasty gravy.

1 kg mutton or lamb, cut into chunks
15 ml garlic and ginger paste
10 ml ground jeera (cumin)
10 ml ground koljana (coriander)
3 pieces stick cinnamon
3 cardamom pods
3 whole cloves
5 ml turmeric (borrie)
10 ml roasted masala
7 ml salt

30 ml sunflower oil
2 large onions, thinly sliced
100 ml water
250 ml grated or finely chopped tomatoes
2 ml sugar (optional)
3 medium potatoes, halved
150 ml hot water
60 ml chopped green dhania leaves
(fresh coriander) (optional)

Wash and drain meat in a colander. Combine with garlic and ginger paste, spices and salt. Heat oil in a large saucepan and braise onions for 5–10 minutes, or until golden brown. Add meat and 100 ml water, and cook over medium heat until meat and spices are well-blended, about 30 minutes. Add tomatoes and sugar, and cook a further 10 minutes, or until tomato is absorbed into gravy. Add potatoes and hot water, and cook until potatoes are soft, about 15 minutes, adding more hot water if a thinner gravy is desired.
Sprinkle with dhania leaves and cook for 2 minutes before serving with Malay rotis (page 47), puri (flat breads) or white rice.

VARIATION
Add 250 ml frozen or canned peas after adding potatoes.

Masala Steak

Tender pieces of steak smothered in a spicy masala sauce.

30 ml sunflower oil	2 ml turmeric (borrie)
2 large onions, thinly sliced	10 ml roasted masala
2 tomatoes, chopped	1 kg rump steak, cut into 10 cm pieces
15 ml garlic and ginger paste	5 ml salt

Heat oil and braise onions until golden brown, about 5 minutes. Add tomatoes, garlic and ginger paste, turmeric and masala, and cook for about 10 minutes, or until well blended. Add steak and salt, and cook, covered, over medium heat until steak is tender, about 30 minutes. Serve with hot chips and vegetable salad.

Malay Rotis

These are lighter and softer in texture than Indian rotis, and are also richer in flavour because they are made with butter.

750 ml cake flour
100 ml self-raising flour
7 ml salt
30 ml sunflower oil
250 ml cold water

100 ml cake flour
100 g butter
50 ml melted butter mixed with
50 ml sunflower oil

Combine cake flour, self-raising flour and salt in a mixing bowl. Add oil, rubbing it into flour to form a crumbly mixture. Add water and mix to a soft dough. Knead, adding extra flour if necessary to make an even-textured, pliable dough. Leave to rest for 30 minutes, covered.

Divide dough into 8–10 pieces. Roll out on a lightly floured surface to a circle 20 cm in diameter, dot with 15 ml butter and sprinkle with flour. Roll and stretch into thick ropes of dough (figure 1). Roll up both ends of the rope, one end clockwise, one anti-clockwise (figure 2) and fold one half flat on top of the other (figure 3). The rotis may be frozen at this stage, interleaved with clingfilm. Leave to rest for 30 minutes, covered.

Roll out on a lightly floured surface to circles about 20 cm in diameter. Heat a heavy-based frying pan and add 5 ml melted butter mixture. Add roti and fry on both sides, brushing with melted butter. Fry until golden brown and speckled. Remove from pan and pat between your palms to fluff surface. Serve hot with curries.

Figure 1

Figure 2

Figure 3

Almond Yellow Rice

A very festive sweet rice to serve with bobotie, sosaties or denningvleis.

500 ml water	5 ml salt
250 ml uncooked long grain rice	50 g blanched almonds
2 pieces stick cinnamon	50 ml sugar
3 cardamom pods	50 g butter or margarine
2 ml turmeric (borrie)	

Bring water to boil. Add rice, cinnamon, cardamom, turmeric and salt, and cook, uncovered, until quite soft, about 20 minutes. Drain in a colander and rinse with hot water. Return rice to saucepan with almonds and sugar, and dot with butter or margarine. Steam, covered, over medium heat for about 10 minutes, stirring lightly every now and then. Add about 50 ml water if rice becomes too dry.

VARIATIONS
Yellow rice with raisins: Add 100 ml raisins, currants or sultanas instead of almonds.
Coconut yellow rice: Add 100 ml desiccated coconut instead of almonds.

MICROWAVE TIP
For fluffier rice, microwave on medium (50%) for about 5 minutes instead of steaming in saucepan.

Vegetable Curry

Any fresh vegetables may be used in this curry.

100 ml sunflower oil

6 small potatoes, peeled

30 ml butter

2 large onions, thinly sliced

2 tomatoes, chopped or puréed

10 ml crushed ginger

5 ml crushed garlic

2 whole fresh green chillies

5 ml chilli powder

5 ml turmeric (borrie)

10 ml ground jeera (cumin)

5 ml ground koljana (coriander)

1.5–2 kg mixed fresh cabbage, carrots, cauliflower, peas and baby marrows

7 ml salt, or to taste

Heat oil in large, deep saucepan and fry whole potatoes over high heat until golden, about 5 minutes. Drain potatoes and set aside. Add butter to oil in saucepan and braise onions until golden, 5–10 minutes. Add tomatoes, ginger, garlic and chillies, and simmer, covered, over medium heat for 15 minutes. Add spices and simmer until well blended, about 10 minutes. Shred cabbage, cut carrots into thin strips and break cauliflower into florets. Add to curry with peas, baby marrows (cut into chunks) and potatoes. Simmer, covered, until the vegetables are tender, about 20 minutes. Add salt to taste. Serve hot with white rice or Malay rotis (page 47).

Tomato and Onion Salad

SERVES 6–8

Chopped dhania leaves make an excellent garnish for this salad.

1 large onion, very thinly sliced
5 ml salt
250 ml warm water
2 large ripe tomatoes, chopped

5 ml crushed dried red chillies or 2 fresh green
    chillies, chopped
30 ml sugar
30 ml white vinegar

Sprinkle onion with salt, and rub it in well. Pour warm water over and leave to drain in a colander. Squeeze out excess moisture. Combine onion with remaining ingredients. Serve as an accompaniment to curries or bredies.

VARIATION
Cucumber and Onion Salad: Use 1 large English cucumber, peeled and grated or chopped, instead of tomatoes.

Orange Baked Pumpkin

SERVES 4

A citrus-tasting side dish to serve with a roast chicken.

500 g pumpkin, cut into chunks
125 g dried peaches or apricots
125 ml fresh orange juice
10 ml brown sugar
1 piece stick cinnamon
25 ml butter

Place pumpkin and peaches or apricots in an oven roasting bag. Cover pumpkin with orange juice, sprinkle sugar over and add cinnamon. Dot with butter and secure bag, piercing a hole near top to allow the steam to escape. Place in an ovenproof dish and bake at 180 °C for 30 minutes, or until pumpkin is tender.

Apple Sambal

Serve this fresh-tasting sambal with a bredie.

3 large Granny Smith apples
5 ml salt
1 fresh green chilli, finely chopped
15 ml lemon juice or white vinegar
20 ml sugar, or to taste

Peel, core and grate apples coarsely, sprinkle with salt and leave juices to draw for 15 minutes. Squeeze out moisture (apple should be fairly dry). Add remaining ingredients and mix well.

Desserts

Bread Pudding

SERVES 6

A rich winter pudding and a good way of using up slightly stale bread.

4 slices white bread, crusts removed
600 ml milk
15 ml custard powder
60 ml sugar
4 extra-large eggs
5 ml vanilla essence
2 pieces stick cinnamon

3 cardamom pods
60 g butter

APRICOT SAUCE (OPTIONAL)
50 ml boiling water
100 ml smooth apricot jam

Cut bread into quarters and soak in 200 ml milk. Mix a little milk with custard powder and 5 ml sugar to form a smooth paste. Heat remaining milk to boiling point.

Add hot milk to custard paste, return to stove and stir to form a thin, runny custard. Beat eggs with remaining sugar and vanilla essence. Add to custard along with remaining ingredients, including bread, and pour into a greased 23 cm diameter ovenproof dish. Bake at 180 °C for 40 minutes. Serve with hot apricot sauce (combine water and jam to form a thin sauce) or *gestoofde droë vrugte* (stewed fruit).

Granny's Favourite Lemon Pudding

SERVES 4–6

A delicious baked lemon pudding. Decorate with lemon leaves before baking for extra flavour.

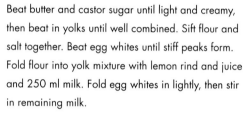

100 g butter
100 g castor sugar
2 extra-large eggs, separated
250 ml self-raising flour
pinch salt
grated rind and juice of 1 large lemon
500 ml milk

Beat butter and castor sugar until light and creamy, then beat in yolks until well combined. Sift flour and salt together. Beat egg whites until stiff peaks form. Fold flour into yolk mixture with lemon rind and juice and 250 ml milk. Fold egg whites in lightly, then stir in remaining milk.

Pour into a well-greased ovenproof dish and bake at 180 °C for 30–40 minutes, or until well-risen. The pudding makes a crusty top with a creamy lemon custard filling.

Easy Pineapple Cheesecake

1 x 80 g packet pineapple jelly
250 ml boiling water
150 ml cold water
1 x 425 g can crushed pineapple
250 ml fresh cream
250 ml smooth cream cheese
1 x 200 g packet Tennis biscuits
125 ml fresh cream and fresh pineapple
or canned pineapple rings for decorating

Dissolve jelly in boiling water, then add cold water and mix well. Set aside to cool. Drain pineapple and reserve liquid. Beat 250 ml fresh cream until thick, add cream cheese and blend well to combine. Add cold jelly and crushed pineapple, and mix well. Dip tennis biscuits into pineapple juice then layer in a square dish. Pour cream cheese mixture over biscuits. Crush remaining biscuits and sprinkle on top. Leave to set in refrigerator for about 1 hour. Beat remaining cream until stiff and pipe on top before serving. Decorate with slices of fresh pineapple or pineapple rings if desired.

Boeber

SERVE 10–12

A thick, spicy milk drink always served hot on the fifteenth night of Ramadan to celebrate the middle of the fast.
For a thicker boeber, add more sago.

100 g butter	75 ml sago, soaked in 200 ml water
250 ml extra-fine, ready-cut vermicelli	for 15 minutes
7 cardamom pods, bruised	100 ml sweetened condensed milk
3 pieces stick cinnamon	15 ml rose-water or 10 ml vanilla essence
50 g sultanas	150 ml sugar, or to taste
2 litres milk	50 g blanched almonds (optional)

Melt butter in a deep saucepan, add vermicelli and toss with a fork until lightly browned. Add cardamom, cinnamon and sultanas, then pour in milk and bring to boil. Stir in presoaked sago and simmer until sago is transparent, about 15 minutes, stirring occasionally to prevent sticking. Mix in condensed milk, rose-water or vanilla essence, sugar and almonds, and simmer until well-blended, about 10 minutes. Serve hot.

Biscuits, Breads and Cakes

Fawzia's Soetkoekies

MAKES 80–100

In the past, sheeptail fat would have been used. Red bolus is a ferri-oxide mixture obtainable from pharmacies.

250 g butter
100 ml sunflower oil
500 ml yellow or brown sugar
5 ml ground cloves
5 ml ground ginger
10 ml ground mixed spice

1 egg, lightly beaten
100 g ground almonds (optional)
500 g cake flour
5 ml bicarbonate of soda
red bolus for colouring
peanut halves for decoration

Cream butter until soft. Stir in oil until well-blended. Add sugar and stir until light and fluffy. Stir in cloves, ginger and mixed spice, then beat in egg. Stir in ground almonds, if using. Sift flour and bicarbonate of soda, and stir into mixture to make a fairly stiff dough.

Mix red bolus with one-third of the dough, until well blended. Roll out remaining two-thirds on a lightly floured surface, dot with pieces of red-coloured dough and roll out to 4 mm thick. Cut into shapes with a biscuit cutter and place on greased baking sheets. Decorate with peanut halves, press in lightly, and bake at 200 °C for 10–12 minutes, or until golden.

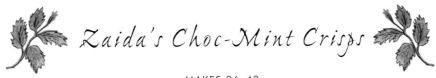# *Zaida's Choc-Mint Crisps*

MAKES 36–40

Crispy chocolate, coconut and mint biscuits that are easy to make.

250 g butter
60 ml sunflower oil
250 ml sugar
50 ml cocoa powder

400 ml desiccated coconut
500 ml cake flour
5 ml baking powder
2 x 50 g peppermint crisp chocolate bars, grated

Cream butter until soft. Stir in oil until well blended. Add sugar and stir until light and fluffy. Stir in cocoa powder and coconut. Sift flour and baking powder, and stir into mixture to make a fairly soft dough. Press into a greased baking sheet and bake at 200 °C for 8–10 minutes, or until golden. Cut into squares while still warm and sprinkle with grated peppermint crisp. Cool before removing from baking sheet.

Cornflakes Biscuits

MAKES ABOUT 150

500 g butter
150 ml sunflower oil
500 g castor sugar
3 large eggs
10 ml ground cardamom

15 ml ground ginger
500 ml chopped dates
100 g walnuts, chopped
1 kg cake flour
500 ml crushed cornflakes

Cream butter until soft. Stir in oil until well blended. Add castor sugar and stir until light and fluffy. Beat in eggs, then stir in cardamom, ginger, dates and walnuts. Sift cake flour and stir into mixture to make a fairly stiff dough. Roll out to 3 mm thick on a lightly floured surface and scrape dough with a fork for a rough texture. Cut out star shapes with a biscuit cutter and coat tops with crushed cornflakes, pressing in firmly with your fingers. Place on greased baking sheets and bake at 200 °C for 10–12 minutes, or until golden.

Koesisters

MAKES 60

Malay koesisters are not plaited, but are oblong in shape, light and puffy, and very spicy.

500 g cake flour
100 ml self-raising flour
100 ml sugar
5 ml salt
10 ml ground ginger
10 ml ground cinnamon
10 ml ground aniseed
5 ml ground cardamom
10 ml ground dried naartjie peel (optional)

100 ml sunflower oil
20 ml instant dried yeast
250 ml cold milk
250 ml hot water
1 egg, beaten
750 ml sunflower oil for deep-frying
1 quantity sugar syrup (see opposite)
150 ml desiccated coconut

Sift flours, sugar and salt into a mixing bowl and stir in spices and naartjie peel. Rub in 100 ml oil to form a crumbly mixture, add yeast and mix to blend well. Mix milk and water and add to flour with beaten egg. Mix to a soft dough. Moisten hands with oil and rub over dough. Set dough aside, covered, to rise until doubled in bulk, about 2 hours.

Roll out dough to a 5 cm thick coil on an oiled surface. Cut off 2 cm lengths and shape each into a slightly flattened oblong shape. Set aside, covered, for 30 minutes to rise again. Heat oil in deep saucepan and fry koesisters for 5 minutes on each side, or until browned. Drain on paper towel or in a colander.

SUGAR SYRUP

500 ml water

375 ml sugar

pinch bicarbonate of soda

10 ml butter

Bring water and sugar to boil until sugar has dissolved and syrup is slightly thickened. Stir in bicarbonate of soda and butter.

Boil koesisters, a few at a time, in sugar syrup for 1 minute, then drain and sprinkle with coconut.

Banana Vetkoekies

MAKES 36

The deeper the oil the more the fritters will puff.

500 ml self-raising flour
pinch salt
15 ml sugar
2 eggs, lightly beaten
30 ml melted butter or margarine
5 ml banana or vanilla essence
200 ml milk

4 large ripe bananas
400 ml sunflower oil for deep-frying
cinnamon sugar

CINNAMON SUGAR
250 ml sugar
10 ml ground cinnamon

Sift flour and salt into a mixing bowl and stir in sugar. Make a well in centre and add eggs, butter, banana essence and milk. Mix to a thick pancake batter. Peel and coarsely chop bananas and add to mixture. Stir to combine well. Heat oil in a large frying pan and drop batter, 15 ml at a time, into it. Fry fritters until golden brown, about 3 minutes on either side. Drain on paper towel.

Cinnamon sugar: Mix sugar and cinnamon together and sprinkle over fritters. Serve hot.

Aniseed Raisin Loaf

MAKES 1 LARGE LOAF

An easy-to-make loaf that doesn't use yeast.

250 ml cake flour
750 ml self-raising flour
pinch salt
10 ml baking powder
20 ml coarsely ground aniseed
250 ml seedless raisins
2 extra-large eggs

125 ml sugar
30 ml sunflower oil
500 ml milk

GLAZE
50 ml sugar
50 ml hot water

Grease and line a large loaf tin. Sift flours, salt and baking powder into a large mixing bowl. Stir in aniseed and raisins. In a separate mixing bowl beat eggs and sugar until light and fluffy, then add oil and beat well. Add flour mixture alternately with milk to egg mixture, mixing after each addition to combine well. Pour mixture into lined loaf tin and bake at 180 °C for 45–55 minutes. Leave in tin for 10 minutes, then turn out onto a wire rack.

Glaze: Dissolve sugar in water and brush over top of raisin loaf. Leave to cool. Serve sliced and buttered.

Cinnamon Carrot Cake

MAKES 1 LARGE CAKE

A popular modern recipe with a cream cheese topping.

250 ml brown sugar
250 ml sunflower oil
4 extra-large eggs, beaten
10 ml ground cinnamon
5 ml bicarbonate of soda
375 ml self-raising flour
7 ml baking powder
350 ml finely grated carrots
100 g walnuts, chopped

TOPPING

250 ml cream cheese
5 ml vanilla essence
25 ml castor sugar

Mix sugar and oil, and stir in beaten eggs. Add cinnamon and bicarbonate of soda. Stir, then add sifted flour, baking powder, carrots and walnuts. Pour into a large, deep, square cake tin and bake at 180 °C for 35–45 minutes, or until a skewer inserted in centre comes out clean. Cool in tin for 10 minutes, then turn out onto a wire rack to cool completely.

Topping: Combine all ingredients well and spread over top of cooled cake.

Hertzoggies

MAKES 60

These traditional Malay cookies are pastry cakes baked with coconut meringue on one side.
When the hertzoggies have cooled apple jelly is spooned over the other side.

250 g butter or margarine	FILLING
60 ml sunflower oil	2 large egg whites
200 ml sugar	150 ml sugar
2 large egg yolks	300 ml desiccated coconut
10 ml lemon essence	300 ml apple jelly or apricot jam
2 ml ground dried naartjie peel	
500 ml self-raising flour	
500 ml cake flour	
pinch salt	

Cream butter or margarine, oil and sugar until light and creamy. Add egg yolks, one at a time, beating well after each addition. Stir in lemon essence and naartjie peel. Sift flours and salt, and mix into creamed mixture to make a very soft dough. Roll out to 6 mm thick on lightly floured surface and cut out rounds with fluted biscuit cutter. Place rounds in greased patty pans.

Filling: Beat egg whites rapidly until stiff, adding sugar gradually. Stir in coconut, mixing well. Spoon 5 ml mixture onto half of each pastry round and bake at 180 °C for 12–15 minutes. Remove from pans and cool on wire rack. When cool, spoon 5 ml apple jelly or apricot jam onto rounds, alongside coconut filling.

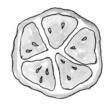

Raisin Tarts

MAKES 2 TARTS

A typical Malay recipe, rich and fruity. The tarts can also be served with cream or custard for dessert.

1 kg ready-made puff pastry or flaky pastry
beaten egg

FILLING
250 ml seedless raisins
250 ml sultanas
60 ml water
30 ml sugar
20 ml butter
10 ml lemon juice

Divide pastry dough in half and roll each out to a round 20 cm in diameter. Use to line 2 pie dishes. Trim off and reserve excess.

Filling: Boil raisins and sultanas in water until plump, about 10 minutes. Add sugar, butter and lemon juice, and cook until nearly dry. Filling should not be watery. Set aside to cool, then spread in pie dishes. Roll out leftover dough, cut into strips and arrange in a lattice pattern over filling. Brush with beaten egg and bake at 220 °C for 10 minutes, then reduce heat to 200 °C and bake a further 10 minutes.

Index

Accompaniments
Almond Yellow
Rice 48
Apple Sambal 53
Malay Rotis 47
Tomato and Onion
Salad 51

Beef
Bobotie 35
Masala Steak 44
Spicy Cottage Pie 39
Biscuits, Breads and
Cakes 62–79
Aniseed Raisin Loaf 72
Banana Vetkoekies 71
Cinnamon Carrot
Cake 75
Cornflakes Biscuits 66
Fawzia's Soetkoekies 63
Hertzoggies 76
Koesisters 68–69
Raisin Tarts 79
Zaida's Choc-Mint
Crisps 65
Biscuits
Cornflakes Biscuits 66
Fawzia's Soetkoekies 63
Hertzoggies 76
Zaida's Choc-Mint
Crisps 65
Cakes
Cinnamon Carrot
Cake 75

Chicken 26–31
Braised Masala
Chicken 27
Chicken Curry 31
Pineapple Peri-Peri
Chicken 28
Curries
Chicken 31
Mutton 43
Vegetable 49
Desserts 54–61
Boeber 60
Bread Pudding 55
Easy Pineapple
Cheesecake 59
Granny's Favourite
Lemon Pudding 56

Fillings
Hertzoggies 76
Raisin Tarts 79
Steak 14
Fish and Seafood
16–25
Egg and Shrimp on
Toast 11
Fish Frikkadels 23
Fried Kabeljou with
Mushroom, Tomato and
Pepper Sauce 18
Haddock Balls 10
Kingklip and Prawn
Paella 17
Pickled Fish 24

Smoorsnoek with
Cabbage 20
Tuna Biryani 25
Lamb
Denningvleis 34
Sosatie Chops 36
Spicy Chops 33

Marinades
Denningvleis 34
Kingklip and Prawn
Paella 17
Sosatie Chops 36
Meat 32–45
Bobotie 35
Denningvleis 34
Masala Steak 44
Mutton Curry 43
Sosatie Chops 36
Spicy Cottage Pie 39
Spicy Lamb Chops 33
Tomato Bredie 40
Mutton
Curry 43
Tomato Bredie 40

Pies
Savoury 14
Potatoes
Mashed 39
Pumpkin
Orange Baked 52

Rice
Almond Yellow 48

Salads
Tomato and Onion 51
Sauces, Savoury
Curry Sauce 24
Mushroom, Tomato and
Pepper 18
Sauces, Sweet
Apricot 55
Sugar Syrup 69
Snacks 8–15
Bhajias 9
Dhaltjies 9
Egg and Shrimp on
Toast 11
Haddock Balls 10
Savoury Pies 14
Spicy Kebaabs 12

Toppings
Bobotie 35
Cinnamon Carrot Cake 75
Cinnamon Sugar 71
Glaze 72

Vegetables and
Accompaniments 46–53
Almond Yellow Rice 48
Apple Sambal 53
Malay Rotis 47
Mashed Potatoes 39
Orange Baked
Pumpkin 52
Tomato and Onion
Salad 51
Vegetable Curry 49